November
Patterns & Projects

Newbridge Educational Publishing, LLC
New York

The purchase of this book entitles the buyer to duplicate
these pages for use by students in the buyer's classroom.
All other permissions must be obtained from the publisher.

©1999 Newbridge Educational Publishing, LLC,
11 East 38th Street, New York, NY 10016. All rights reserved.

ISBN: 1-58273-127-6

Table of Contents

Cornucopia Art Project 5
   Fall Harvest Graph 9
   Cornucopia Memory Game 10
   Tasting Party 11

How to Make the Over the River File-Folder Game 12
   Over the River File-Folder Game 13
   Over the River and Through the Wood 17
   Then and Now 18

Squirrel Paper-Bag Puppet 19
   A Squirrel Song 23
   Home-School Squirrel Note Bag 24
   Hide-and-Seek Nuts 25

Autumn Mural 26
   Chipmunk Sorting 30
   Scarecrow Compound Word Activity 31
   Four-Season Class Discussion 32
   The Five Senses of Autumn 33
   Fall Fun 34

Thanksgiving Stick Puppets 35
   Thanksgiving Poem 38
   Native American Symbols 39
   Recommended Reading 41
   Native American Creative Writing 41

Native American Costume 42
   Native American Name Game Song 46
   Native American Class Discussion 47
   Recommended Reading 47

How to Make the Is This Thanksgiving? File-Folder Game ... 48
   Is This Thanksgiving? File-Folder Game 49
   Matching Feathers 53
   My Book of Holidays 53
   How Many Feathers? 54

Thanksgiving Cards 55
   Thanksgiving Mobile 55
   Beginning Blends 59
   Making Butter 59
   Thanksgiving Topsy-Turvy Table 60

Thanksgiving Books 61
   All About Turkeys 62

Table of Contents (Continued)

Favorite Thanksgiving Foods Survey 66
An Autumn Walk 66

Thanksgiving Centerpieces **67**
Thanksgiving Math 71
We Are Grateful 72

Why Trees Tremble in the Wind Flannel Board Story **73**
How to Make the Flannel Board 74
Native American Village 74
Cinderella Story Class Discussion 78
Guessing Game 79

Teacher's Notes **80**

Art/Small Motor Skills

CORNUCOPIA ART PROJECT

You need:
- crayons or markers
- scissors
- stapler
- tissue or newspaper
- 3" x 3" sheet of butcher paper
- tape

1. Reproduce the cornucopia patterns on pages 6 through 8 four times. Have groups of children color two sets.
2. Help children cut out all the figures. Then match one colored figure along with a corresponding plain figure and staple together around the edges, leaving a small opening, as shown.
3. Have children stuff the openings with crumpled tissue or newspaper and staple closed.
4. Cut a large sheet of butcher paper into an 8" x 8" square. Let children color the paper on both sides.
5. Fold the square into a cone shape, as shown, and tape together.
6. Fill the cornucopia with the fruit and vegetable figures. Display the cornucopia on a table in a reading corner along with books about the fall season, farming and harvesting, fruits and vegetables, etc.

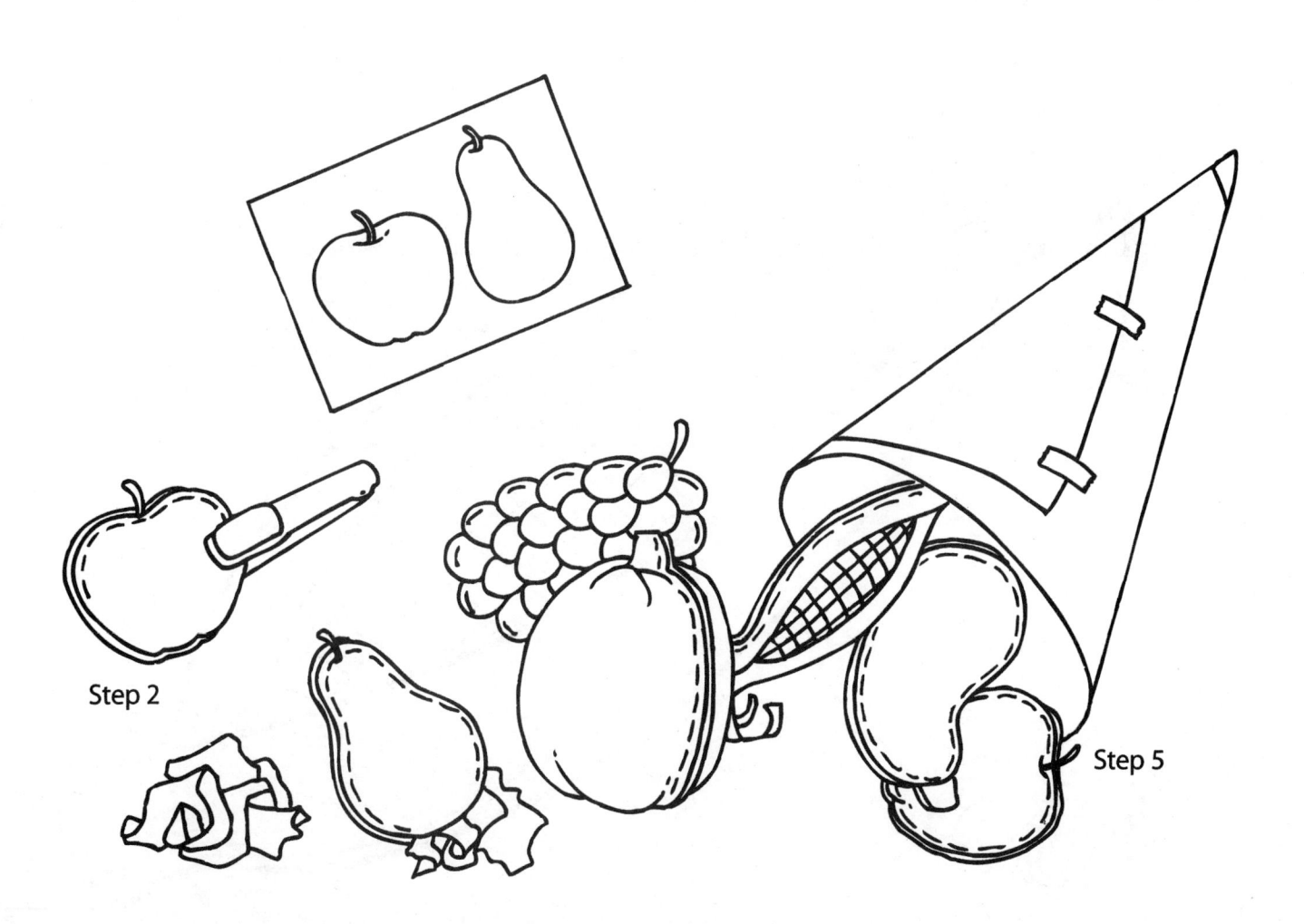

Step 2

Step 5

Vegetable Patterns

Newbridge

6

Vegetable and Fruit Patterns

Newbridge

Fruit Patterns

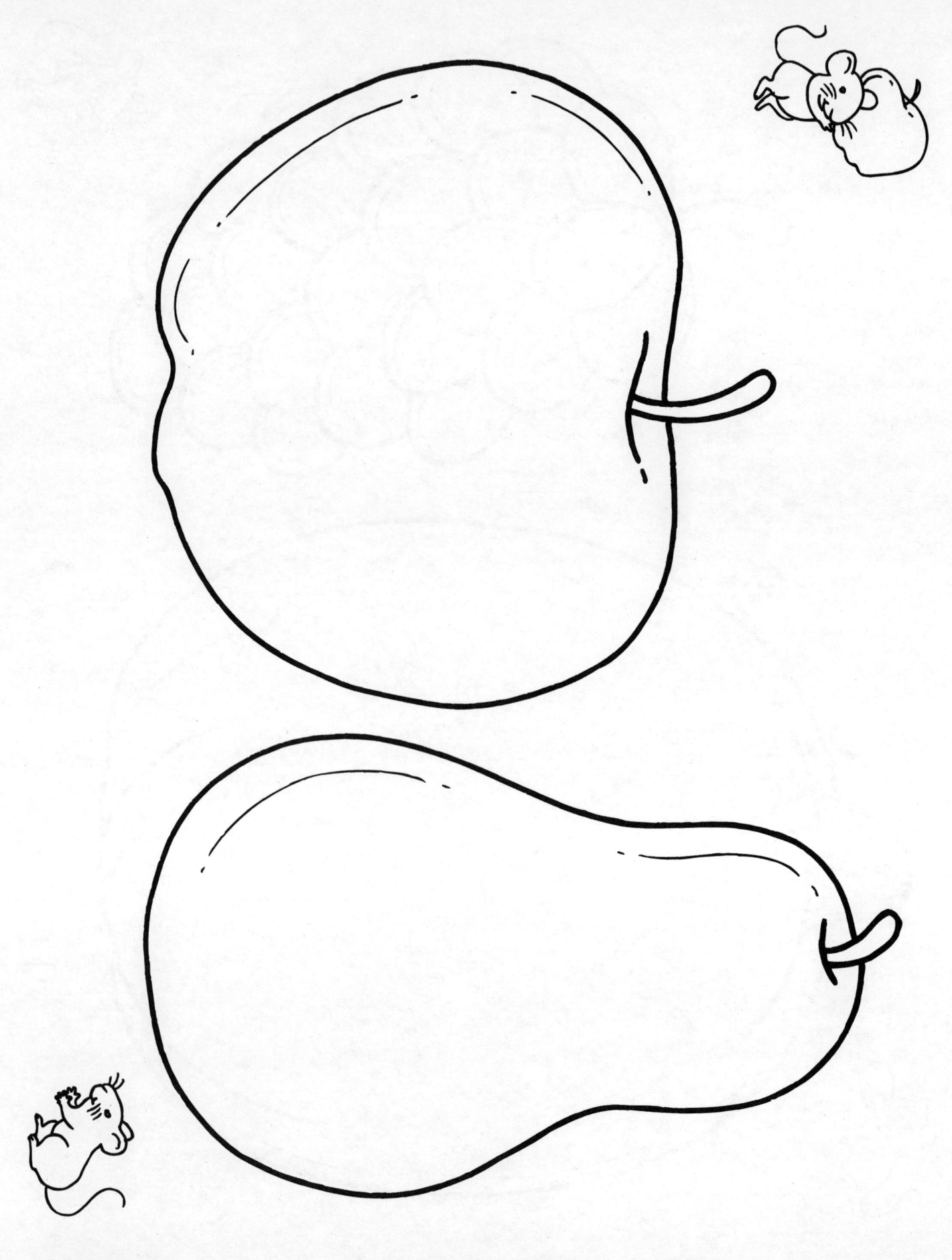

Newbridge

8

Math/Graphing/Sorting/Counting

FALL HARVEST GRAPH

You need:
- crayons or markers
- scissors
- pushpins or tacks

1. Reproduce the cornucopia patterns on pages 6 through 8 once. Color and cut out.
2. Write the name of the fruit and vegetable on each figure. Then make two horizontal rows on a bulletin board. Label one row "Vegetables" and the other "Fruits," as shown.
3. Spread the pictures out on a large table for children to see.
4. Ask volunteers to come up and attach each figure to the correct row on the bulletin board.
5. Ask a volunteer to tell how many vegetables there are. Ask another volunteer to tell how many fruits there are. Are there more fruits or vegetables on the bulletin board? How many fruits and vegetables are there altogether?
6. Ask children to make drawings of other fruits and vegetables. Then have children come up to the bulletin board and place their drawings in the appropriate rows.

9

Memorization Skills/Visual Discrimination

CORNUCOPIA MEMORY GAME

1. Take several fruits and vegetables from the cornucopia and arrange them in a circle or in rows on a table.
2. Have a small group of children sit in a circle around the display and look carefully at it. Then ask the children to turn their backs and hide their eyes.
3. Choose one child to add or to remove one object from the display.
4. The other children may then turn around and try to figure out what has been changed.

Comparing and Contrasting/Observation

TASTING PARTY

You need:
- canned pumpkin
- grapes (green and red seedless)
- apples (various kinds)
- pears
- canned corn
- table knives
- paper plates
- plastic spoons

Optional:
- oaktag
- pushpins or tacks

1. Help children cut the fruits and vegetables into small pieces and place on paper plates.
2. Ask children to observe and comment upon the differences and similarities in texture, color, size, shape, etc.
3. Give each child a paper plate. Let children select different kinds of fruits and vegetables to taste. Encourage children to taste unfamiliar items as well as favorites.
4. Have a discussion with children after the tasting party. Talk about how the fruits and vegetables look, taste, smell, and feel. Encourage the use of descriptive words such as *sweet*, *sour*, *bumpy*, and so on.
5. Have children name other foods eaten in the fall and around Thanksgiving. If desired, write the words on a large piece of oaktag and attach it to a wall or a bulletin board.

Art/Small Motor Skills/Following Directions

HOW TO MAKE THE OVER THE RIVER FILE-FOLDER GAME

You need:
- crayons or markers
- scissors
- glue
- letter-sized file folder
- oaktag
- envelope
- different-colored construction paper
- clear contact paper
- die

1. Reproduce the game board on pages 14 and 15 once and the game cards on page 16 eight times. Color the game board and cut out.
2. Mount the game board on the inside of a letter-sized file folder, as shown.
3. Reproduce the game instructions on page 13. Color, cut out, and mount on the front of the file folder.
4. Mount the game cards on oaktag and color four sets. Cut apart the colored sets.
5. Glue an envelope to the back of the file folder to store the cards.
6. Cut a 1" square from each of four different colors of construction paper. Laminate to use as markers.

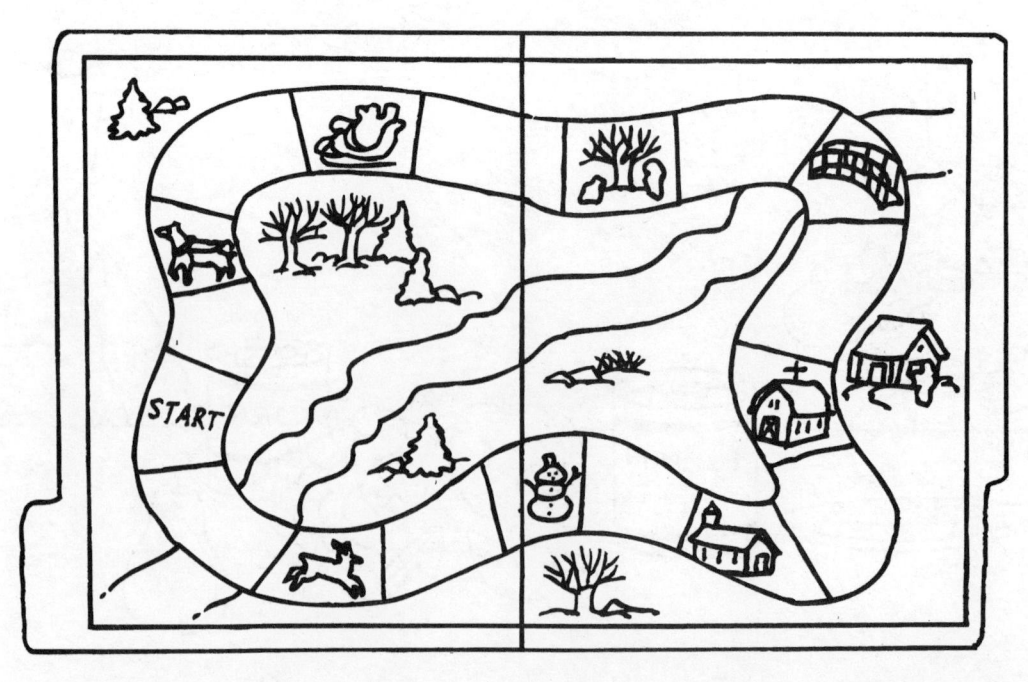

Following Directions/Matching

OVER THE RIVER FILE-FOLDER GAME

How to Play
(for 2 to 4 players)

1. Place the colored game cards faceup near the game board. Each player takes one set of uncolored game cards.
2. Each player places his or her marker on "Start." The youngest player goes first and rolls the die.
3. That player moves the indicated number of spaces clockwise or counterclockwise. If the player lands on a picture space, he or she takes the matching picture from the pile and covers the matching space on the board of uncolored game cards. If a player lands on a blank space, he or she does nothing.
4. Play continues clockwise. If a player lands on "Start," he or she may take another turn.
5. The winner is the first player who has collected all nine objects on the way to Grandmother's house and covered all the spaces on the board of uncolored game cards.

START

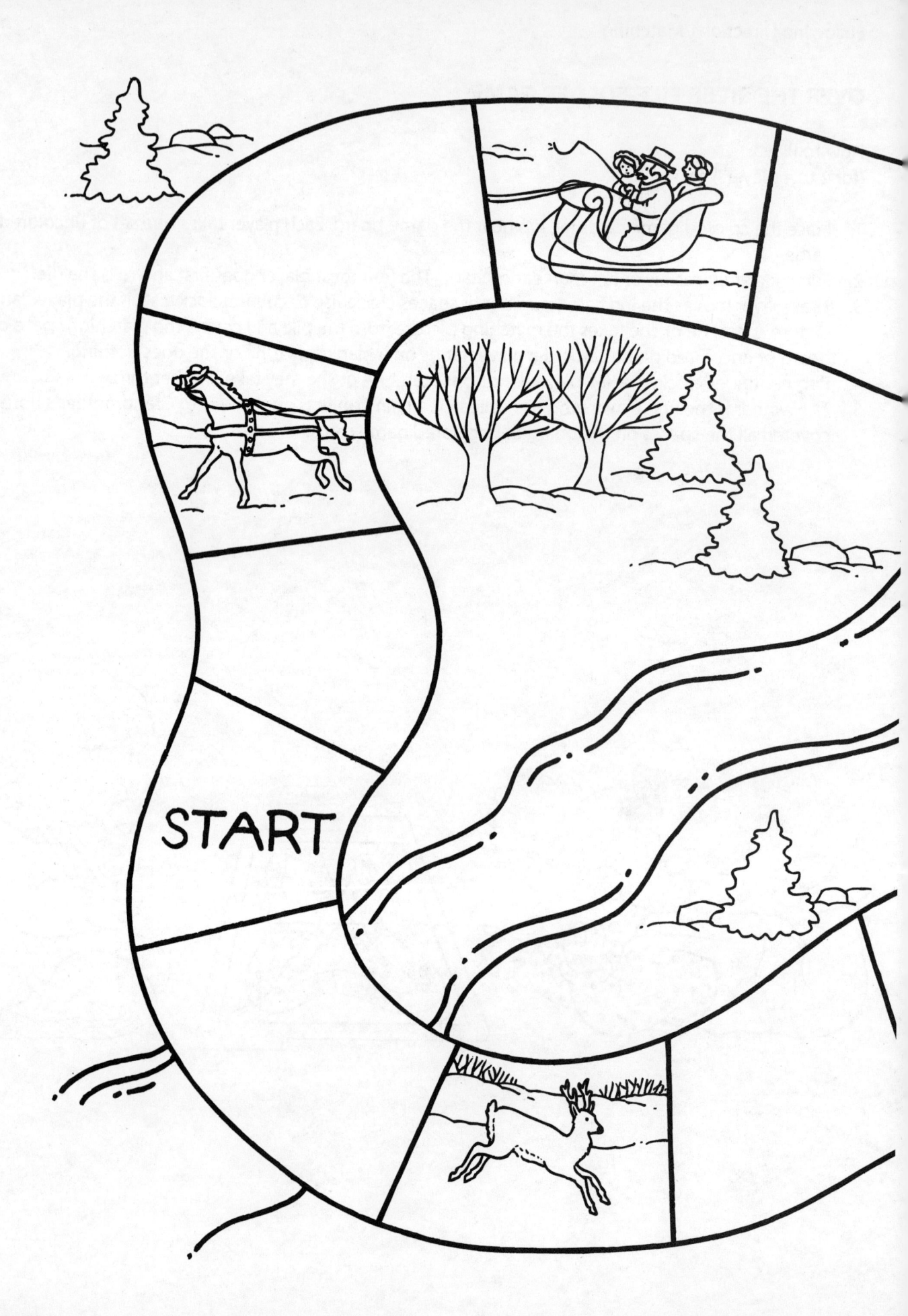

Newbridge

Newbridge 15

Over the River Game Cards

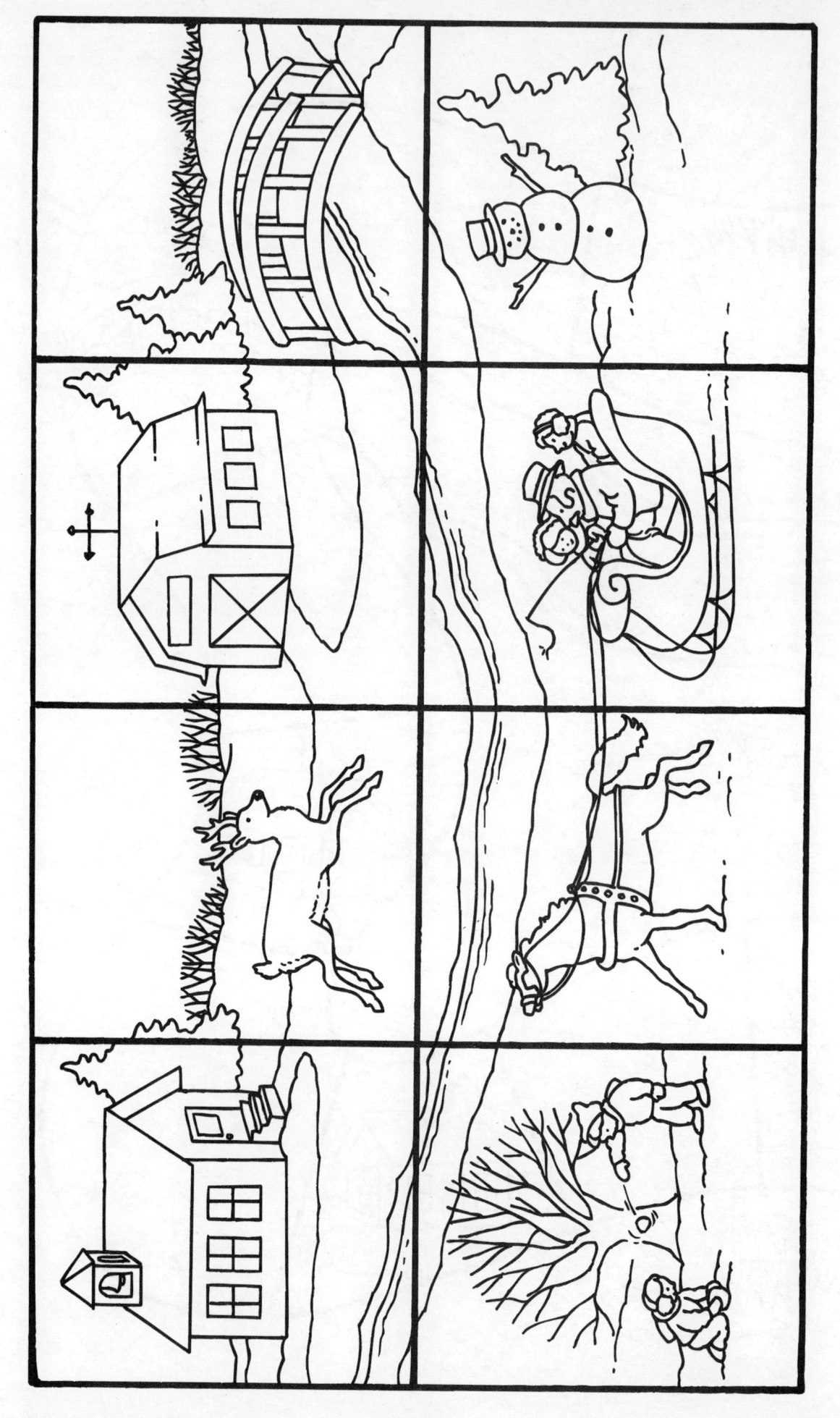

Newbridge

Literature Connection/Dramatic Play/Large Motor Skills

OVER THE RIVER AND THROUGH THE WOOD
by Lydia Maria Childs

Teach the following song and accompanying actions to the class at Thanksgiving.

Over the river and through the wood,
To Grandmother's house we go.
(*children make hands go up and down in a zigzag motion*)

The horse knows the way to carry the sleigh,
Through the white and drifted snow.
(*children pretend to hold reins*)

Over the river and through the wood,
(*repeat first motion*)
Oh, how the wind does blow!
(*children move hands in front of faces, back and forth*)

It stings the toes and bites the nose
As over the ground we go.
(*children touch toes, then noses*)

Over the river and through the wood,
(*repeat first motion*)
Trot fast my dapple gray!
(*children pretend to hold reins*)

Spring over the ground like a hunting hound,
For this is Thanksgiving Day!
(*children bounce hands up and down*)

Over the river and through the wood,
(*repeat first motion*)
Now Grandmother's face I spy!
(*children shield eyes with hands, as if saluting*)
Hurrah for the fun! Is the pudding done?
(*children wave hands in air*)
Hurrah for the pumpkin pie!
(*children rub stomachs*)

Thinking Skills/Social Skills

THEN AND NOW

1. After teaching children "Over the River and Through the Wood" on page 17, explain to the class that this song was written a long time ago, and that many things have changed in the world since that time.
2. Discuss food, houses, clothing, leisure activities, and customs from the olden days compared to now. Remind children that there was no electricity when this song was written. What are some differences one might expect because of this? Explain that a lot more work had to be done by hand, and people didn't have as much spare time as they do now. But because there was no television or radio or video, people often played together in the evenings.
3. Divide a piece of chart paper into two columns. Label one column "Then" and the other column "Now." Ask children to list things that might be appropriate to the columns, based on the previous discussion.
4. Invite an elderly visitor to come and tell the class about what Thanksgiving was like when he or she was young. Of course, that person will not be as old as the song is! Have children compare Thanksgiving customs from years ago to Thanksgiving customs today.

Art/Small Motor Skills/Following Directions

SQUIRREL PAPER-BAG PUPPET

You need:
- crayons or markers
- scissors
- glue
- brown paper lunch bags

1. Reproduce the squirrel patterns on pages 20 through 22 for each child. Have children color and cut out.
2. Demonstrate to the class how to glue the squirrel head to the bottom of a lunch bag, and the body and bundle of nuts to the front of the bag, as shown.
3. Help each child glue the tail to the back of the bag.
4. Show each child how to place his or her hands in the bag and curl his or her fingers around the bottom so that when the child moves his or her fingers, it looks like the squirrel's head is moving.
5. For activities, see A Squirrel Song on page 23.

Step 2

Step 3

Squirrel Puppet Patterns

Newbridge

Squirrel Puppet Pattern

Newbridge

Squirrel Puppet Pattern

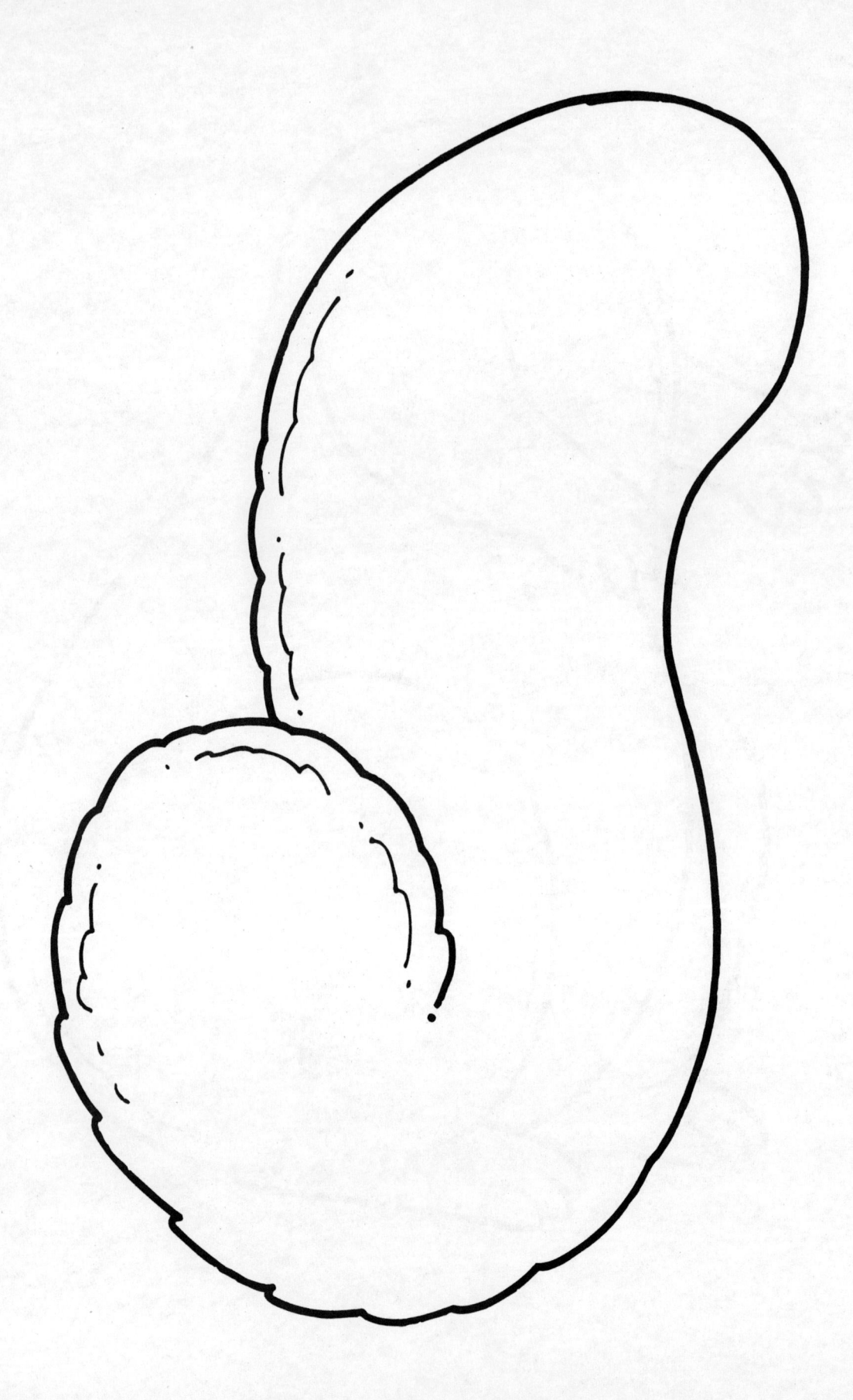

Newbridge

Science/Dramatic Play/Large Motor Skills

A SQUIRREL SONG
(sung to the tune of "She'll Be Coming Round the Mountain")

Teach the class the following song about squirrels with accompanying movements. Have children use their squirrel puppets when acting out the song.

I'll be gathering all the acorns till they're gone.
I'll be gathering all the acorns till they're gone.
I'll be gathering all the acorns, gathering all the acorns,
Gathering all the acorns till they're gone.
(*children make collecting motions with hands*)

And I'll put them all inside my little home.
I will put them all inside my little home.
I will put them all inside, put them all inside,
Put them all inside my little home.
(*children pretend to place nuts in tree house*)

And I'll eat the nuts until the winter's gone.
I will eat the nuts until the winter's gone.
I will eat the nuts until, eat the nuts until,
Eat the nuts until the winter's gone.
(*children pretend to eat acorns*)

Then I'll do it all again come next fall.
I will do it all again come next fall.
I will do it all again, do it all again,
Do it all again come next fall.
(*children make gathering motion with hands and arms again*)

Home-School Connection

HOME-SCHOOL SQUIRREL NOTE BAG

1. Reproduce the squirrel head, body, and tail patterns on pages 20 through 22 four times. Have volunteers color and cut out.
2. Glue the head to the body at the neck, and the tail off to one side of the body, as shown.
3. Open a paper lunch bag and stand it upright. Then glue a squirrel to one side of the bag so its feet are even with the base of the bag, as shown. Repeat with the other squirrels on other lunch bags.
4. With a heavy black marker, write the category of notes to be held in each squirrel note holder. Some suggestions are: field trip permission slips, school board and P.T.A. meetings, parent-teacher conferences, and materials needed for special projects.
5. Attach the bags securely to a board or wall. Introduce the Notes for Home Center to the class and explain that notices for parents will be placed in the appropriate bags.
6. When parents come to the classroom to pick up their children, have them look in the message center and take any notices for that day. If parents do not come to the classroom, have children check the message center before they leave for the day and place the appropriate notices in their book bags.

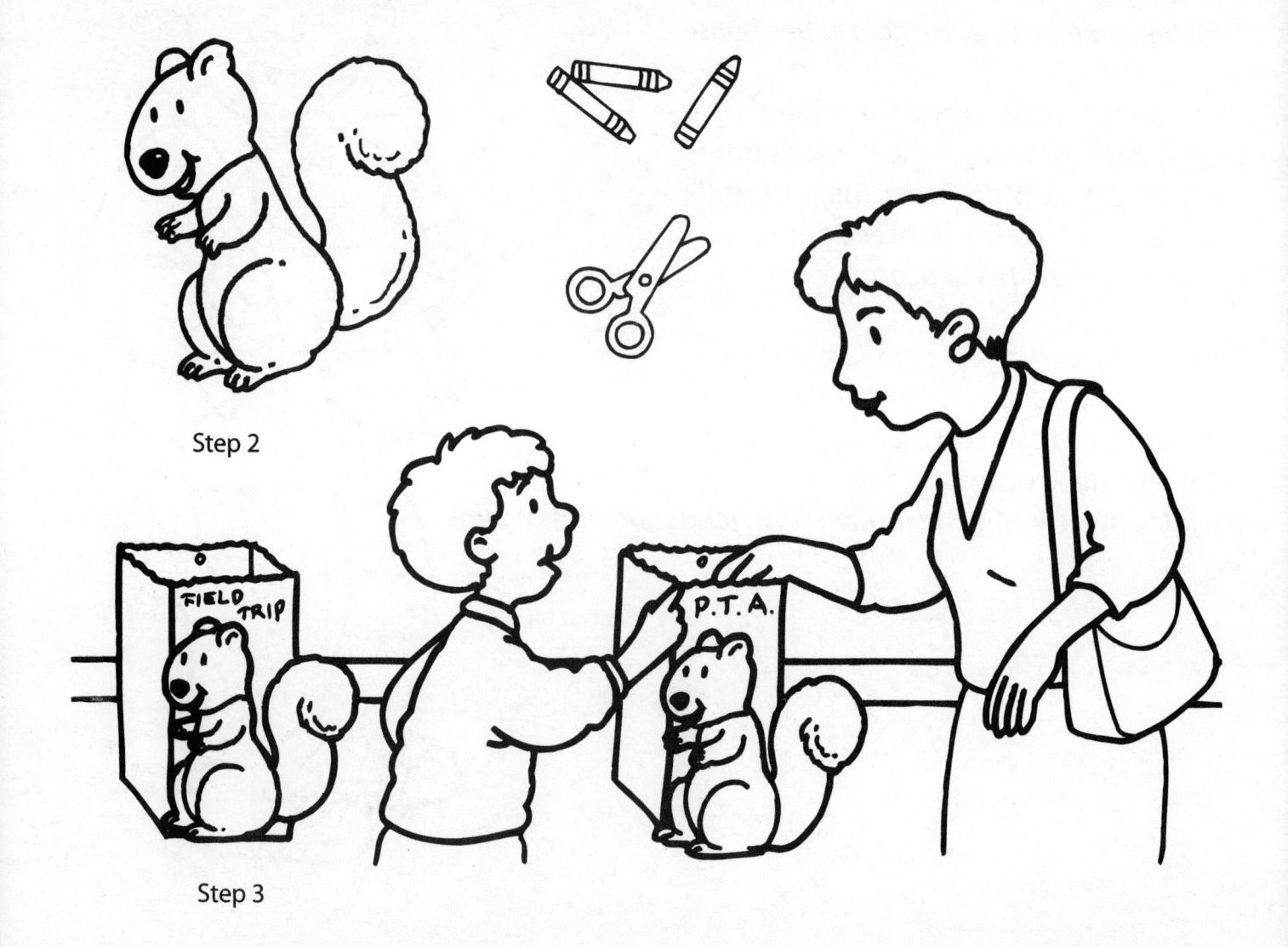

Step 2

Step 3

HIDE-AND-SEEK NUTS

This squirrel is hiding nuts to be eaten in winter. Circle all the nuts you find.

Name _____

Newbridge

25

Art/Small Motor Skills

AUTUMN MURAL

You need:
- crayons or markers
- scissors
- newspaper
- tape
- large sheet of butcher or bulletin paper
- assorted paper scraps and other collage materials
- glue

1. Reproduce the autumn patterns on pages 27 through 29 several times. Color and cut out.
2. Choose a floor area for the mural that is away from classroom traffic. Cover the area with newspaper and tape the butcher paper over it.
3. Provide children with paper scraps, assorted collage materials, and glue.
4. Divide the class into five groups: grass, trees, pond, sky, and weather. Children may wish to gather real leaves and twigs from outdoors to add to the mural.
5. When the background is finished, have children decide where to place the children, scarecrow, and chipmunks, then glue in place.
6. Hang the mural on a classroom wall for all to enjoy.

Autumn Pattern

Newbridge

Autumn Pattern

Newbridge 28

Autumn Pattern

Newbridge

Sorting/Thinking Skills/Art/Small Motor Skills

CHIPMUNK SORTING

1. Reproduce the chipmunk pattern on page 29 several times. Have volunteers color and cut out.
2. Staple or tape a large sheet of bulletin board paper to a classroom wall or bulletin board. Glue the chipmunks 5" apart along the middle of the paper, as shown.
3. Glue a pocket under each chipmunk. On each pocket, write a word to describe a category, such as "Toys," "Clothing," "Animals," "Machines," "Food," or "Homes." If possible, add a picture to illustrate each word. For example, if the pocket under one chipmunk reads "Toys," tape a picture of a toy in the chipmunk's front paws or nearby.
4. Have children look for pictures illustrating these words in old magazines or workbooks and cut out. Place these in a separate pocket (pockets may be made to resemble acorns) near the display area.
5. Children may come to the display board one at a time, pick a picture, and then place it in the matching pocket. Or, children may wish to play with a partner during free time.

Thinking Skills/Word Recognition

SCARECROW COMPOUND WORD ACTIVITY

1. Reproduce the scarecrow and crow pattern on page 28 ten times. Reproduce the crow ten more times. Have volunteers color and cut out the scarecrows.
2. Cover a bulletin board with blue paper along the top and green along the bottom. Make the green paper resemble cornstalks, as shown.
3. Attach the scarecrows to the board so they stand a little above the cornstalks. Staple a Velcro tab on each scarecrow's hands.
4. Glue Velcro tabs to the backs of small index cards. Attach a crow to each card, as shown. On each pair of crows, write one half of a compound word. For example, you may write "cup" on one crow and "cake" on the other.
5. Ask volunteers to read the words on each card, or have the words read to them. Then let children place each half of the compound word in a scarecrow's hands. Continue until all the crows have been paired with their matching half.
6. This game may also be played using any theme having pairs, such as homonyms, antonyms, synonyms, rhymes, or categories.

Science/Critical Thinking/Comparing and Contrasting

FOUR SEASON CLASS DISCUSSION

1. Divide the class into four groups: autumn, winter, spring, and summer. Ask each group to bring clothing that represents their season.
2. Display the clothing on a table. Discuss the thickness, color, texture, fabric, and why each article is good for a particular season. Have children point out differences and similarities between the articles of clothing. Ask children how they would feel wearing a heavy sweater in summer or a bathing suit in winter.
3. Talk about the current season and the clothing the class is wearing that day.
4. Assign partners and give each pair four pieces of clothing that represent the four seasons. Have them order the clothes according to season, beginning with fall and ending with summer.
5. Next, give partners clothing for different parts of the body and have them construct an "invisible" person on the floor using the clothes.
6. Lastly, choose a season and lay out an outfit for that season with one inappropriate piece of clothing. Have children tell which article of clothing is inappropriate and why. Continue for each season.

Critical Thinking/Graphing/Sorting

THE FIVE SENSES OF AUTUMN

1. Show children a collection of objects that suggest autumn and have them discuss how they perceive these things through their five senses. For example, you may want to show apples, nuts, pinecones, and dry leaves. Encourage children to add to the collection.

2. Make a graph by drawing a picture of each of the five senses along the left side of a large piece of oaktag. Draw pictures of items discussed across the top from left to right. Then have children color in squares on the graph for each sense that is used. For example, if the item were an apple, a child would color in the squares for seeing, touching, tasting, and smelling.

3. Ask children to observe autumn outdoors, both at home and at school. Have children add to the graph and color in squares each time they see, hear, smell, taste, or touch something related to autumn.

FALL FUN

Name _____

Circle the five things in the picture on the left that are different from the things in the picture on the right. Then color the pictures.

34

Newbridge

Art/Small Motor Skills

THANKSGIVING STICK PUPPETS

You need:
- crayons or markers
- scissors
- construction paper
- craft sticks
- glue

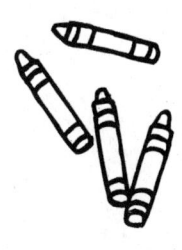

1. Let each child choose one of the figures on pages 36 and 37 to make a stick puppet. Reproduce the selected figure once for each child. Have children color and cut out.
2. Have children trace the figures onto construction paper and cut out.
3. Next, have children lay the front of each puppet on top of its construction paper back.
4. Help children place craft sticks between the fronts and backs of the puppets.
5. Have children glue the fronts and backs of the puppets together.
6. For activities, see Thanksgiving Poem on page 38.

Thanksgiving Stick Puppet Patterns

Newbridge   36

Thanksgiving Stick Puppet Patterns

Newbridge

37

Social Studies/Dramatic Play

THANKSGIVING POEM

Divide the class into two groups: Native Americans and Pilgrims. Teach each group their part of the following poem. Let children use their stick puppets as they speak.

Pilgrims: Where do we start? What do we do?
We have just come to this land that's new.

Indians: We have lived in this country for very long.
We'll show you how our villages got to be strong.

Pilgrims: If you show us some things, we'll learn very fast.
We'll work together to build a town that will last.
But your kindness and help we will never forget.
We will always remember the day that we met.

Both: Let's have a feast. We'll sing and play,
And give thanks that we're able to share in this way.

Social Studies/Thinking Skills/Creative Writing

NATIVE AMERICAN SYMBOLS

You need:
- crayons or markers
- scissors
- glue
- blank index cards
- construction paper
- pushpins or tacks

1. Reproduce the Native American symbols on page 40 four times. Color and cut out.
2. Mount the symbols on blank index cards.
3. Hold each symbol up in front of a small group of children. Explain that Native Americans spoke and wrote differently than we do now. When the Pilgrims settled, they had to communicate with the Native Americans by using their hands and drawing pictures. Most of the early Native American languages were written in pictures.
4. Ask children to tell what they think the symbols mean. Explain that Native Americans named themselves after things in nature that had special meaning for them (for example, Blue Sky, Swift Bird, Dances with Wolves, and so on). Write the actual meanings on each card.
5. Let each child choose his or her own Native American name. Give each child a piece of construction paper. Then ask children to draw a picture of what the symbol for their names might be.
6. Have each child write or dictate his or her Native American name at the bottom of each picture. Attach the symbols to a bulletin board. Title the board "Our Native American Names."

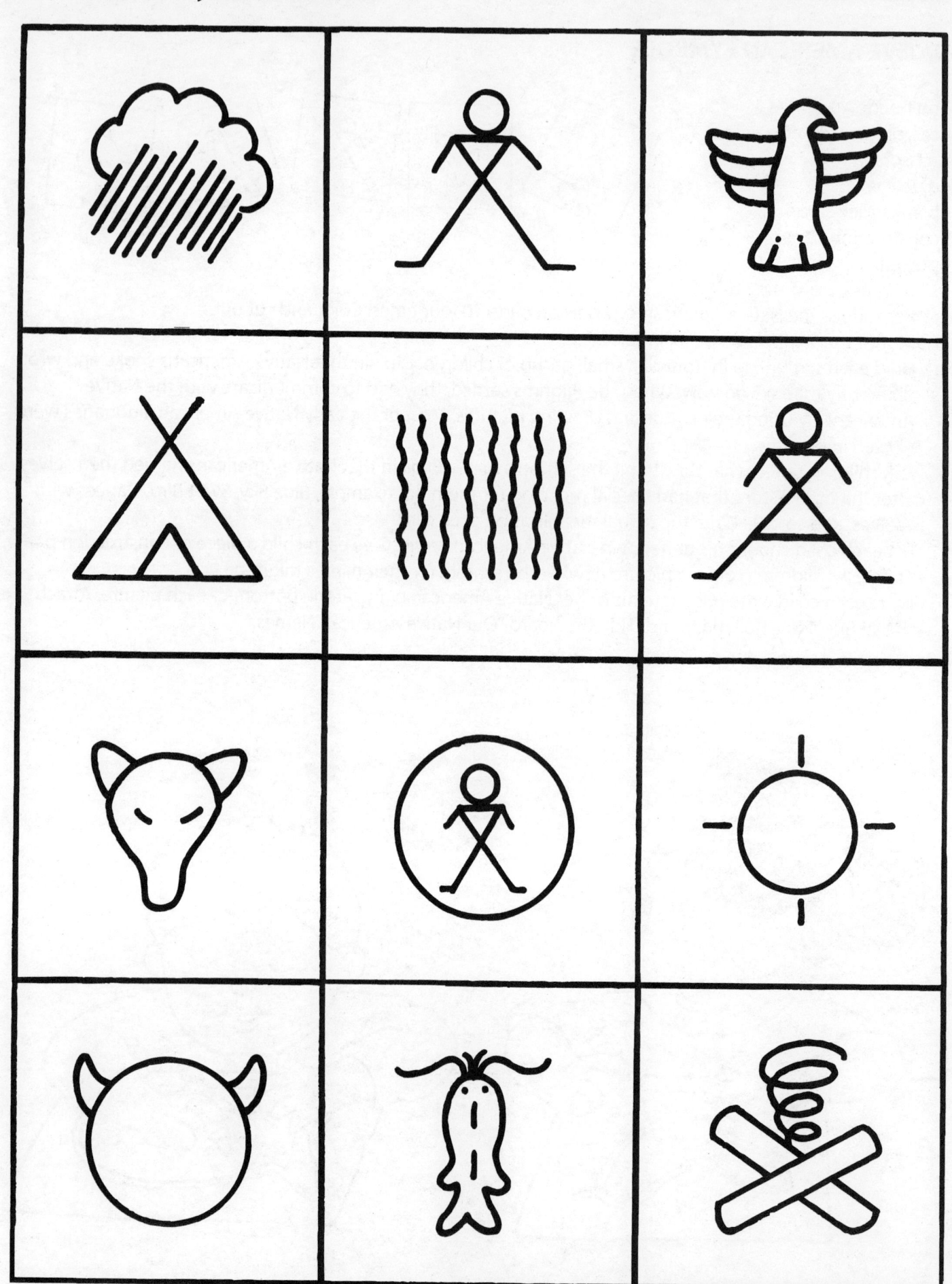

Native American Symbol Patterns

Newbridge

Creative Writing/Literature Connection

RECOMMENDED READING

Read some of the following books about Native Americans to your class. Place the books on a reading table or in a bookcase so that children may look at them during free time.

Bright Fawn and Me by Jay Leech and Zane Spencer, published by HarperCollins.
Good Hunting, Little India by Peggy Parish, published by HarperCollins.
Indian Two Feet and the ABC Moose Hunt by Margaret Friskey, published by Children's Press.
Indian Two Feet Rides Alone by Margaret Friskey, published by Children's Press.
Little Chief by Syd Hoff, published by HarperCollins.
Red Fox and His Canoe by Nathaniel Benchley, published by HarperCollins.

NATIVE AMERICAN CREATIVE WRITING

1. Divide the class into small groups. Give each group a complete set of symbols.
2. Ask each group to write or dictate a story using the symbols.
3. When all the stories have been completed, ask each group to share their story with the rest of the class.
4. If desired, let children illustrate their stories. Place the stories on a reading table so that children may look at them during free time.

Art/Small Motor Skills

NATIVE AMERICAN COSTUME

You need:
- crayons or markers
- scissors
- large brown grocery bags
- collage materials
- 3" x 12" strips of brown construction paper
- stapler
- glue

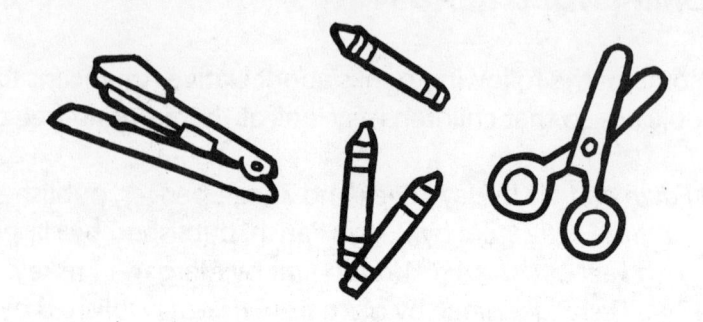

1. Reproduce the headpiece and symbol patterns on pages 43 and 45 once and the moccasin pattern on page 44 twice for each child. Have children color and cut out.
2. Help each child cut out a circle from the bottom of a grocery bag. The circle should be large enough for his or her head to fit through. Then show children how to cut slits up the narrow sides of the bag to make armholes.
3. Have children fringe the bottom of the bag by making cuts 1" apart, as shown. Have children finish decorating the bag using collage materials and Native American symbols.
4. Show each child how to staple two strips of brown construction paper together and fold in half lengthwise. Attach the headpiece pattern to the strip, as shown. Staple to fit around each child's head. Children may also wish to decorate their headpieces using collage materials.
5. Help each child fold another strip of brown construction paper in half lengthwise and glue the center of it to the top of each moccasin, as shown. Staple to fit around each child's ankles.
6. For activities, see Native American Name Game Song on page 46.

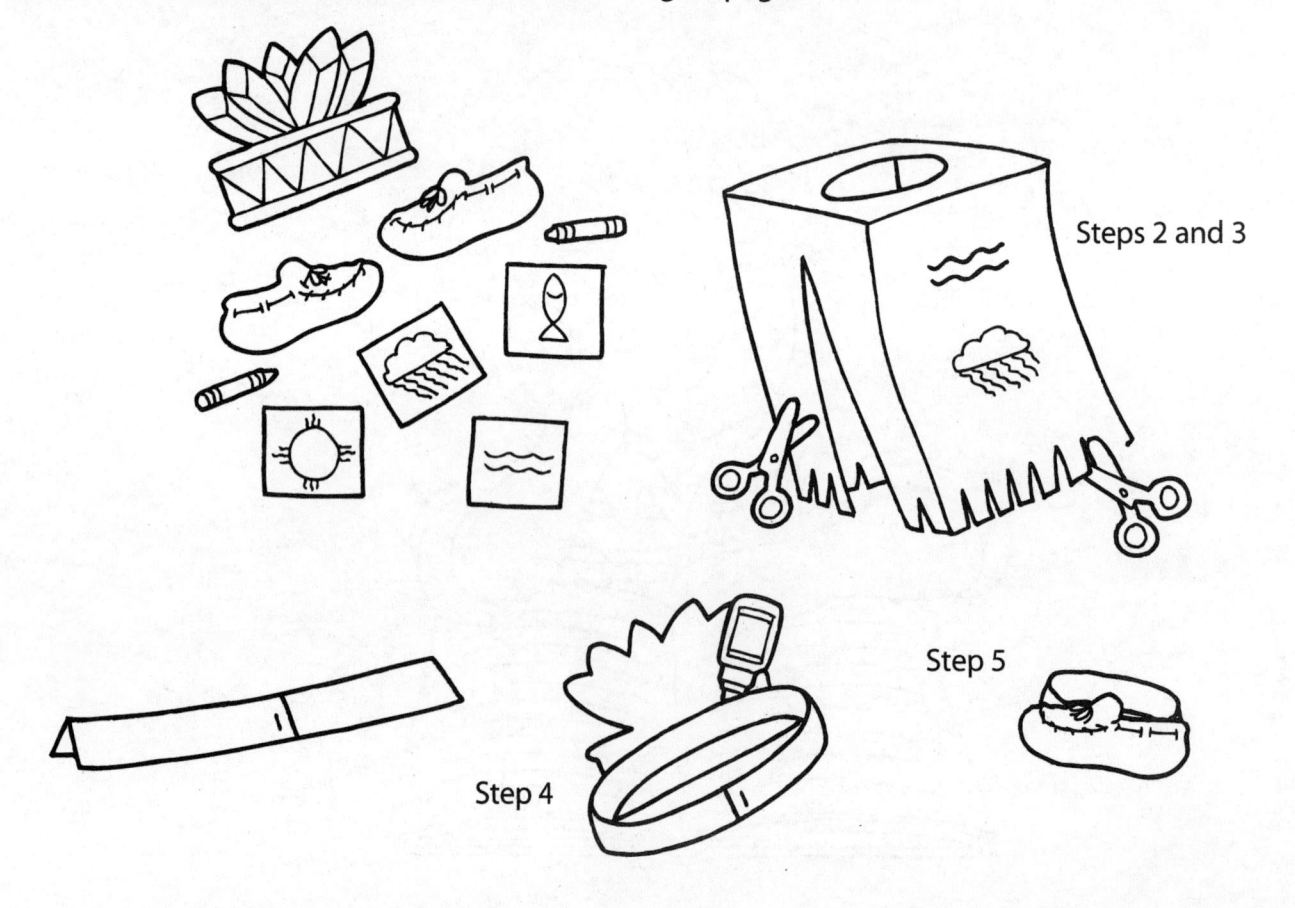

Steps 2 and 3

Step 4

Step 5

Native American Costume Pattern

Newbridge

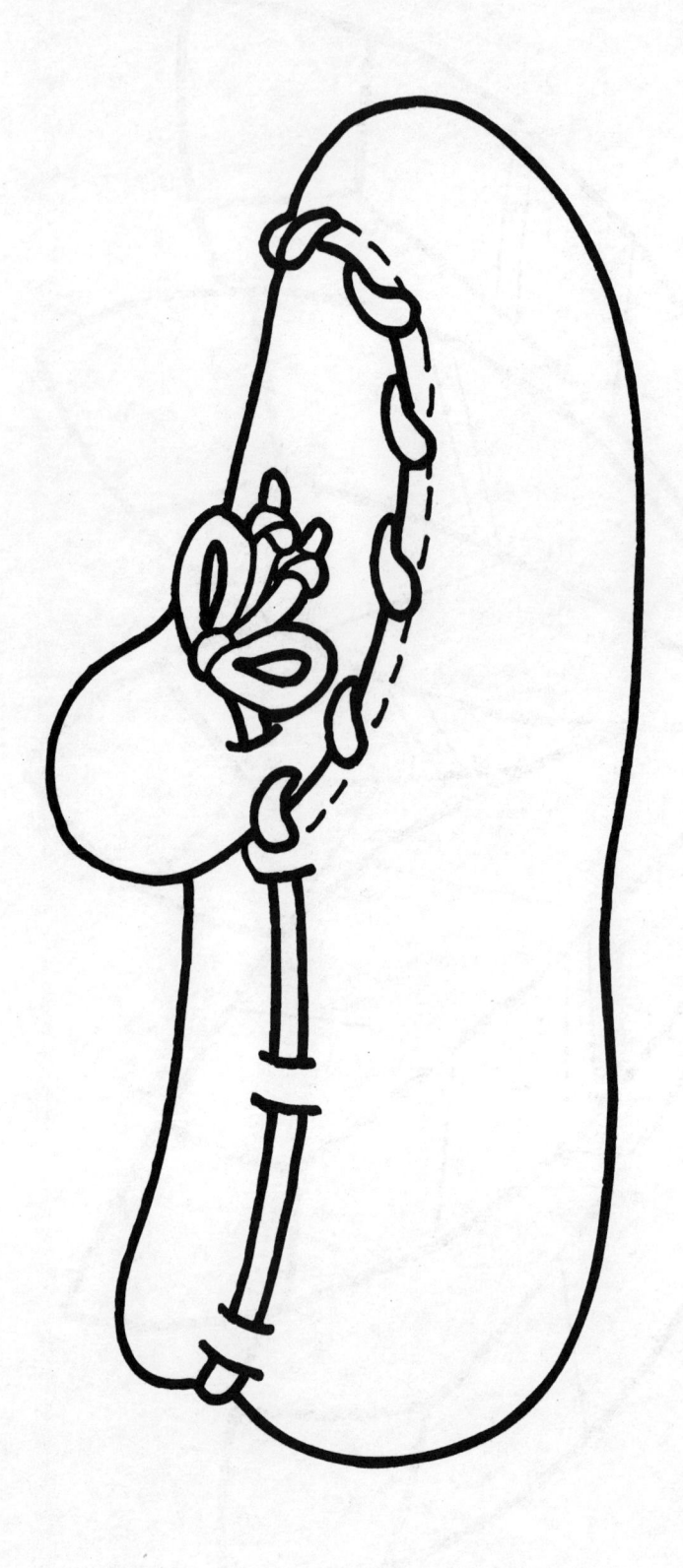

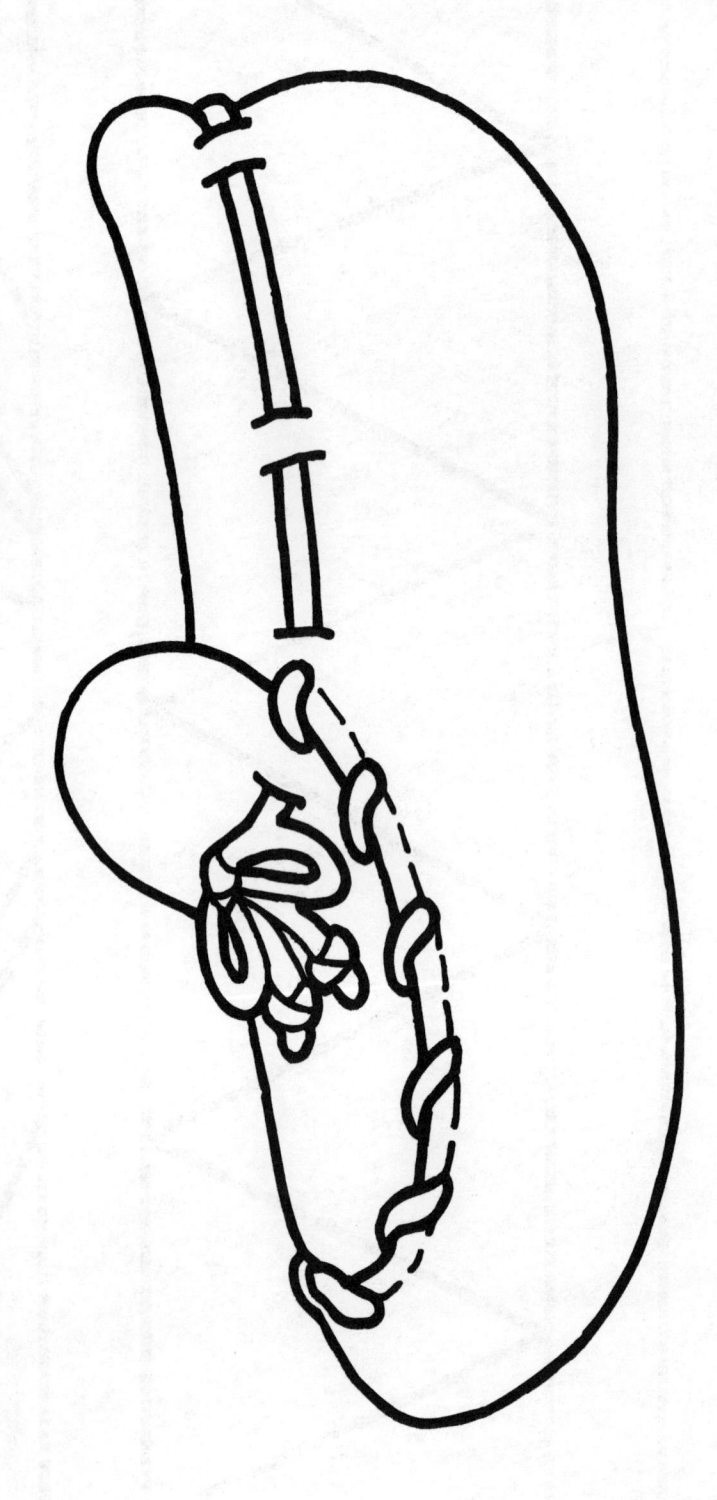

Native American Costume Pattern

Newbridge 44

Native American Symbols Pattern

Large Motor Skills/Dramatic Play

NATIVE AMERICAN NAME GAME SONG
(sung to the tune of "Where Is Thumbkin?")

Before playing this game, ask volunteers to name some of the Native American names they have heard and read (for example, "Flying Bird"). Explain the significance and meaning of Native American names. Then ask each child to choose a Native American name for himself or herself. Have the class sit in a circle wearing their Native American costumes as they sing the following song.

Where is Flying Bird?
Where is Flying Bird?
(*children sing song as teacher calls out selected Native American name*)

Here I am.
Here I am.
(*child with selected name sings*)

Show us what your name means.
Show us what your name means.
(*class sings*)

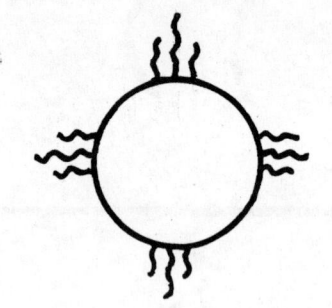

Here I go.
Here I go.
(*child pretends to fly around like a bird*)

Social Studies/Critical Thinking/Literature Connection

NATIVE AMERICAN CLASS DISCUSSION

Ask children if they understand the term "Native American." Explain that it describes the people who lived in America before Europeans and other settlers arrived in North America. Point out on a world map or globe a route early settlers might have taken from their own native land to America. Ask children which lands are native to their first ancestors who came to America.

Discuss with children what Native American life might have been like, in the woods or out on the plains, long ago. Remind the class that there were no malls or roads or telephones as we have now. Ask them to think of what kinds of houses Native Americans might have had (different tribes had different types of homes); what kinds of food they ate (meats, vegetables, and grains) and how they got it (hunting and farming); what children might have done for fun (there were many games, such as lacrosse); and how they got their clothing (made out of animal skins).

Emphasize the respect for nature that is important to Native American culture. Tell the class that tribes who lived in different areas of America had different customs and ceremonies for various phases of life and nature: the harvest, illness, the weather, marriage and birth, decision-making, and leadership.

Ask children to wear their Native American costumes and hold a "council meeting." Explain that these meetings were how Native Americans made decisions about their lives. Give children a decision to make concerning the activities of the day, the naming of a class pet, or a field trip idea, and allow time for everyone to express an opinion. Then after they have talked a lot, let the majority rule.

RECOMMENDED READING

Read some of the following books about Native American folktales to the class. Place the books on a reading table or in a bookcase so that children may look at them during free time.

Brother Eagle, Sister Sky: A Message from Chief Seattle, published by Dial.
Buffalo Woman by Paul Goble, published by Simon & Schuster.
The Gift of the Sacred Dog by Paul Goble, published by Bradbury Press.
The Legend of the Bluebonnet by Tomie de Paola, published by Putnam.
Small Wolf by Nathaniel Benchley, published by HarperCollins.
Where the Buffaloes Begin by Olaf Baker, published by Viking.

Small Motor Skills/Following Directions

HOW TO MAKE THE IS THIS THANKSGIVING? FILE-FOLDER GAME

You need:
- crayons or markers
- scissors
- glue
- letter-sized file folder
- oaktag
- different-colored construction paper
- clear contact paper
- envelope

1. Reproduce the game board on pages 50 and 51 and the game instructions on page 49 once. Reproduce the game cards on page 52 three times. Have children color and cut out the game board.
2. Glue the game board to the inside of a file folder, as shown.
3. Mount the game cards on oaktag. Color and cut out.
4. Cut 1" squares from four different colors of construction paper. Laminate to make playing pieces.
5. Glue an envelope to the back of the file folder. Use the envelope to store the playing pieces and game cards.

Symbol Recognition/Critical Thinking/Following Directions

IS THIS THANKSGIVING? FILE FOLDER GAME

How to Play
(for 2 to 4 players)

1. The oldest player goes first and play continues clockwise.
2. Place the playing pieces at "Start." Place the game cards facedown in the center of the turkey on the file folder.
3. The first player picks a card from the top of the game-card pile and decides whether or not the symbol on the back represents the Thanksgiving holiday. If the player guesses correctly, he or she moves ahead one feather; if not, he or she stays in place.
4. The first player to reach the finish wins.

START

FINISH

Newbridge 51

Is This Thanksgiving? Game Card Patterns

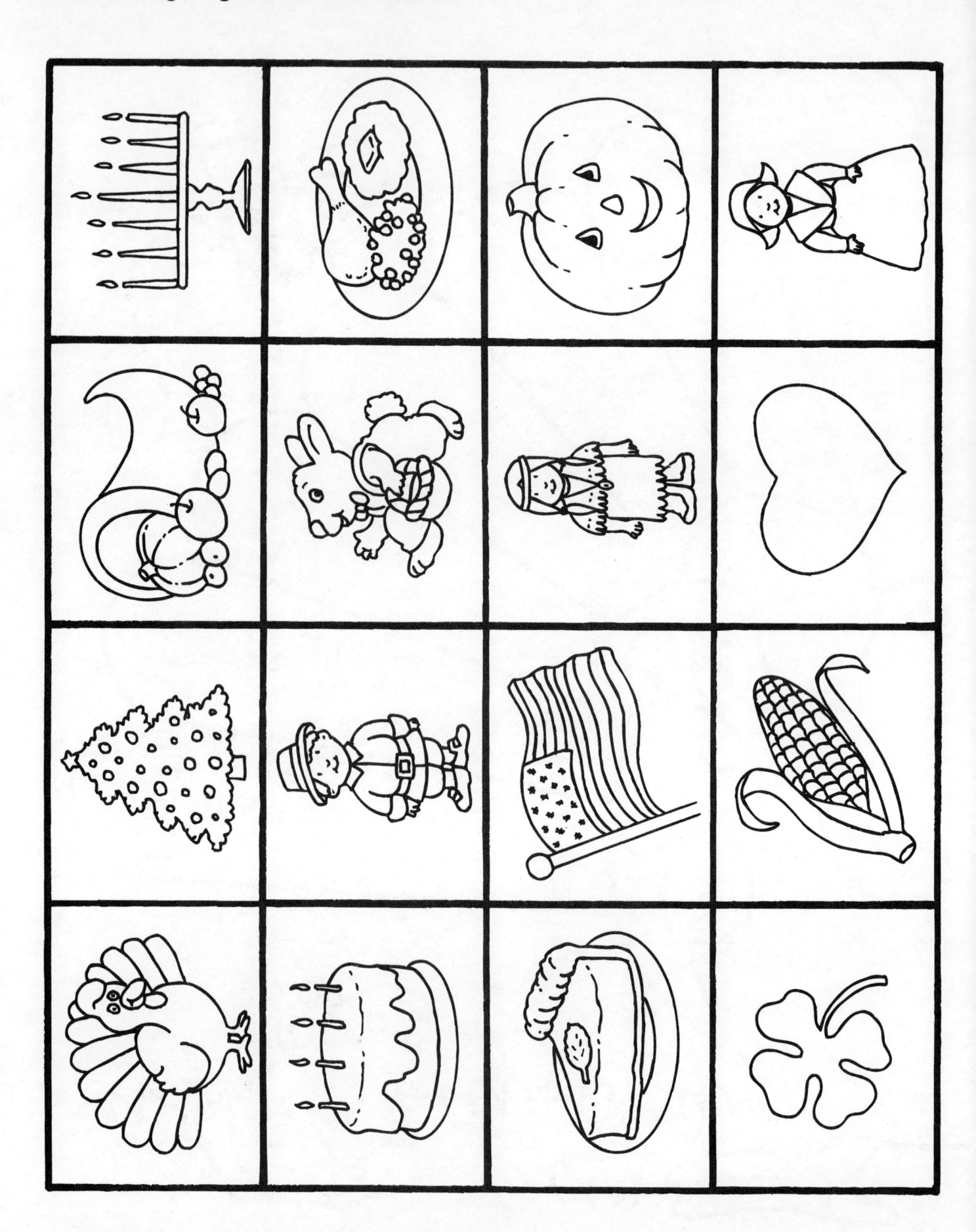

Newbridge 52

Matching/Letter and Number Recognition/Writing/Art/Small Motor Skills

MATCHING FEATHERS

1. Reproduce the turkey pattern on pages 50 and 51 three times. Have volunteers color, mount on oaktag, and cut out.
2. Cut the feathers off the turkey. On the body of the turkey, write an uppercase letter. Write the matching lowercase letter on several feathers, and other lowercase letters that are similar in appearance on the rest of the feathers.
3. Repeat with other turkeys, using a different letter for each.
4. Place each turkey and set of feathers in a file folder. Write the uppercase letter and the matching lowercase letter in large print on the cover of each folder.
5. During free time, let children place feathers around the turkey body that show the matching lowercase letter. Children may check their answers by looking at the cover of the folder.
6. For additional challenges, have children match objects and weather to their seasons, math equations to numbers, pictures to letters, dots to numbers, and coin combinations to cent amounts.

MY BOOK OF HOLIDAYS

1. Reproduce the game cards on page 52 once for each child. Have children color and cut out one Thanksgiving card and all the non-Thanksgiving cards.
2. Have each child make a book of holidays by gluing each game card to a piece of construction paper. Ask children to draw pictures of other things that are appropriate for each holiday. For example, if the card featured is the Christmas tree, a child might want to draw pictures of Santa Claus, presents, elves, and so on.
3. Ask each child to write or dictate a sentence telling what he or she likes best about each holiday. For example, a child might want to say, "My favorite thing about Christmas is seeing my cousins."
4. Encourage children to make covers for their books. Have children write "My Book of Holidays" on the covers.
5. Show children how to staple the pieces of construction paper together along the left side to complete their books.

HOW MANY FEATHERS?   Name _____

Count the feathers on each turkey. Write the numbers on the lines provided. Then color the pictures.

_____   _____

_____   _____

Newbridge

Home-School Connection/Writing/Art/Small Motor Skills/Following Directions/Oral Communication

THANKSGIVING CARDS

You need:
- crayons or markers
- glue
- scissors
- construction paper
- stapler
- decorating materials: glitter, yarn, tissue paper, cotton balls

1. Ask each child to choose a pattern on pages 56, 57, or 58 to use for a Thanksgiving card. Reproduce the selected pattern once for each child. Have children mount on oaktag and cut out.
2. Help children trace the patterns onto colored construction paper and cut out. Children may then write or dictate Thanksgiving messages on the construction paper and sign their names.
3. Show children how to attach the two pieces of the card together by stapling along the left side.
4. Give children decorating materials, such as glitter, yarn, tissue paper, and cotton balls, to use to personalize their cards.
5. Let children bring their Thanksgiving cards home to give to a friend or relative.

THANKSGIVING MOBILE

1. Reproduce all the patterns on pages 56 through 58 for each child. Have children color and cut out.
2. Give each child a 2" x 18" strip of oaktag and pieces of yarn 6", 8", 10", and 18" in length.
3. Help each child punch a hole at the top of each figure and tie one end of the 6", 8", and 10" lengths of yarn to each hole.
4. On the back of each figure, have each child write or dictate a sentence telling what that symbol means to him or her.
5. Have children staple the ends of the strips of oaktag together to form a circle. Then help children punch three holes in their strips, evenly spaced, and tie the loose ends of the yarn to each hole, as shown.
6. Have children punch two more holes in the oaktag strip, as shown, and tie the ends of the 18" length of yarn to each hole. Use this loop to hang the mobiles around the classroom.
7. Ask children to draw a picture (or pictures) showing what they are thankful for on Thanksgiving. Have them attach their pictures to the mobile. If desired, let each child explain to the rest of the class why he or she wanted to add the picture.

Turkey Pattern

Pilgrim Pattern

Newbridge

Native American Pattern

Newbridge

Letter and Sound Recognition/Reading/Blends/Social Studies/Following Directions

BEGINNING BLENDS

1. Reproduce the Pilgrim boy pattern on page 57 and the Native American girl pattern on page 58 five times. Have volunteers color and cut out.
2. Place the figures on a bulletin board so that children can see them. Then write the letters *TH* on ten small index cards. Tack the index cards to the figures, as shown.
3. Tell the children the sound *TH* makes. Explain that this sound is called a blend because it blends the sounds of two letters, *T* and *H*
4. Ask volunteers to think of words that begin with the *TH* sound (for example, *thanks*, *Thanksgiving*, *this*, *that*, *there*, *think*, and so on). Write the endings of the suggested words on small index cards and place them on the bulletin board next to the cards on the figures to show the complete words, as shown.
5. Review a new blend each week by changing the index cards on the figures. Other suggested blends are: *BR, CR, DR, FR, FL, SL, SP, ST,* and *WH*.

MAKING BUTTER

1. Explain to the class that long ago, when the first settlers came to America, there were no stores where people could go to buy butter. The settlers had to make it themselves. Discuss where children think butter comes from or is made. Then tell children they will be making butter the way early settlers did, from the milk of a cow.
2. In a covered container, pour a pint of heavy cream. Add a teaspoon of salt. Close the lid securely.
3. Demonstrate to the class how to shake the container up and down in a vigorous manner. Then have children take turns shaking the cream for as long as they can last.
4. When the cream is hard, the butter is ready. Put out crackers and bread, plastic knives, and the butter. Help children butter their bread and enjoy.

Name _____

THANKSGIVING TOPSY-TURVY TABLE

This is a topsy-turvy Thanksgiving dinner table! There are six things wrong with this picture. Circle the topsy-turvy things, then color in the picture.

Newbridge

Art/Small Motor Skills/Writing/Home-School Connection

THANKSGIVING BOOKS

You need:
- crayons or markers
- scissors
- glue
- construction paper
- hole puncher
- short lengths of yarn or metal notebook rings

Optional: library pocket and index card

1. Let each child choose one of the patterns on pages 63 through 65 to use to for a book cover. Reproduce the selected pattern twice for each child.
2. Have children color, cut out, and mount on construction paper.
3. Help each child trace his or her pattern on construction paper five times and cut out. These will be the pages of the book.
4. Allow children to choose book titles. Have children write their names as the authors on the cover.
5. On the inside pages, tell children to make pictures on a Thanksgiving theme, such as the first Thanksgiving or Thanksgiving dinners in their own homes. Have children write or dictate sentences describing their illustrations.
6. After children have finished working on the pages, help them stack the papers in order between the front and back covers of each book. Children may want to add an "About the Author" page to their books.
7. Punch three holes along the left side of each book, as shown. Help children thread lengths of yarn through the holes and tie together to complete their books.
8. Place the books in a reading area for children to enjoy during their free time, or allow children to check out the books to take home by gluing a library pocket and index card in each book. After everyone has enjoyed the books, let each child take his or her book home to share with family members.

Science/Critical Thinking/Research

ALL ABOUT TURKEYS

1. Reproduce the turkey pattern on page 63 once. Color and cut out.
2. Glue the turkey to the center of a sheet of oaktag or chart paper.
3. Divide the space around the turkey into three parts. Label the left part "What We Know," the middle part "Questions We Have," and the right part "What We Learned."
4. Have children sit in a group facing the turkey chart. Ask them what they already know about turkeys, such as "Turkeys have feathers" and "Turkeys are big." Write their comments in the left area of the chart.
5. Next, ask children if they have questions about turkeys, such as "Do turkeys have teeth?" or "Can turkeys fly?" Write the questions in the middle area of the chart.
6. Read the children an entry from an encyclopedia or an animal book that has information about turkeys.
7. After children have heard the information about turkeys, read their questions back to them. Were any of these questions answered? If so, write the new information in the right area of the chart.
8. Check the children's original statements. If any facts were found not to be true, review the information and ask children to correct it by writing the new information they have learned in the right area of the chart.
9. Give each child a turkey-shaped sheet of paper and have the children write or dictate something new they learned about turkeys.

Turkey Pattern

Newbridge 63

Leaf Pattern

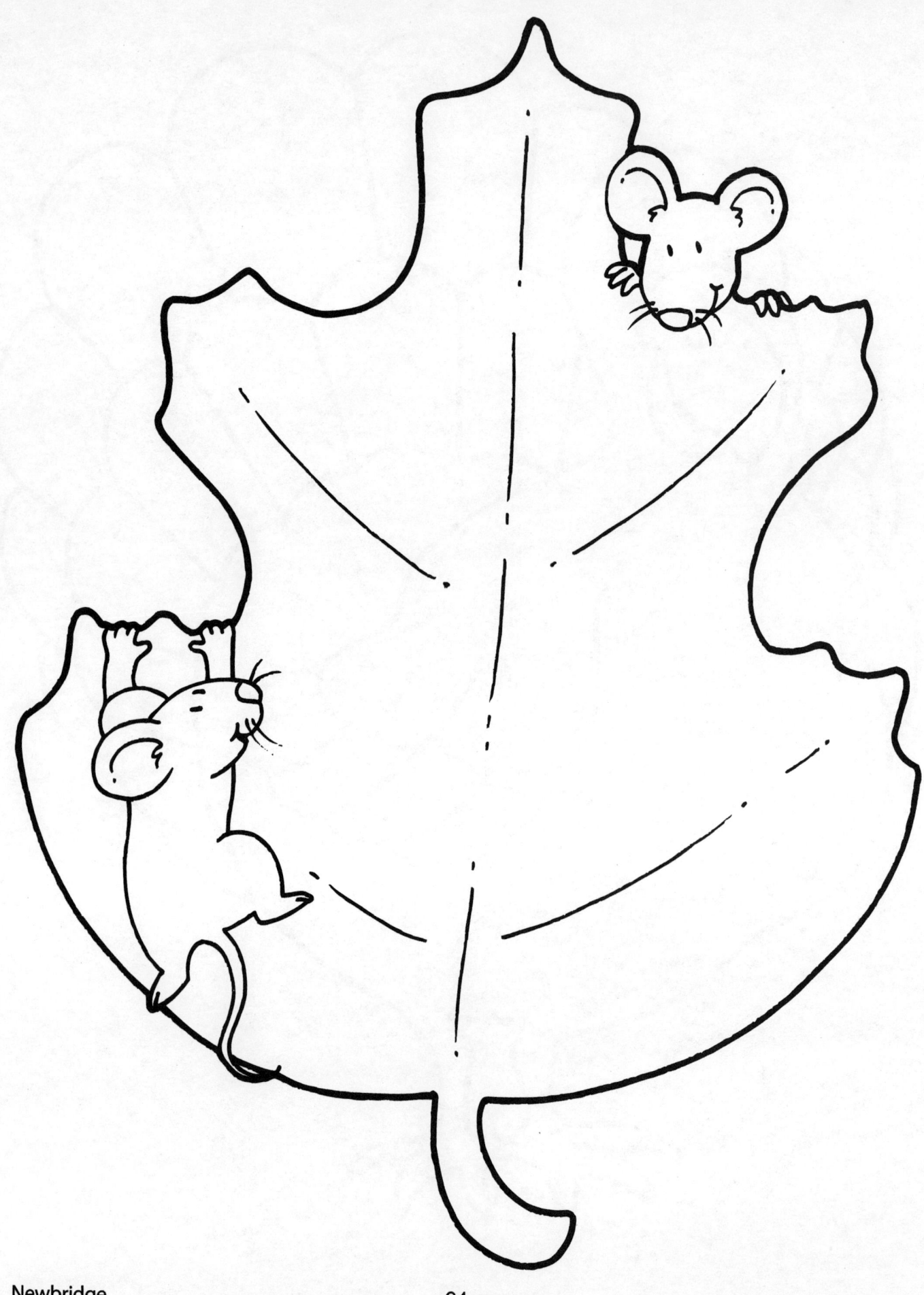

Newbridge 64

Cornucopia Pattern

Newbridge 65

Graphing/Thinking Skills/Writing/Observation

FAVORITE THANKSGIVING FOODS SURVEY

1. Discuss with children the types of foods they like to eat at Thanksgiving dinner. List the foods on a large piece of oaktag.
2. Make a graph by listing the foods on a large cornucopia-shaped sheet of paper, as shown. Help children color squares next to the foods they like.
3. Divide the class into groups of two or three children each. Assign each group one of the foods.
4. On sheets of cornucopia-shaped paper, have each group write or dictate something about the food (such as where it is grown or raised) and tell how it might be prepared. Ask each group to tell why that food is associated with Thanksgiving.
5. Make a cornucopia book by stapling the pages together in order of a food's popularity, with the most popular food first, and the least popular last.

AN AUTUMN WALK

1. Invite children to go for an autumn walk, asking them to watch and listen for the sights and sounds of autumn.
2. Take a walk, stopping on occasion to enjoy the beautiful weather. If desired, collect leaves, acorns, and other nature finds for a fall display.
3. When the walk is over, have the children describe some of the things they saw and heard. Write their words on a sheet of oaktag or chart paper.
4. Ask each child to make a page for an Autumn Walk Book about what he or she experienced outdoors. Have children write or dictate and illustrate their work.

Art/Small Motor Skills

THANKSGIVING CENTERPIECES

You need:
- oaktag
- glue
- crayons or markers
- scissors
- empty, clean half-gallon milk containers
- sand
- colored tissue paper
- adhesive tape
- glitter, stickers, colored paper scraps, etc.

1. Have children choose their favorite Thanksgiving pattern on pages 68 through 70. Reproduce the selected pattern once for each child. Have children mount on oaktag, color, and cut out.
2. Give each child an empty half-gallon milk container (filled with a small amount of sand) and colored tissue paper. Have children tape the tissue paper around the carton, covering it entirely.
3. Have children glue their Thanksgiving patterns to one side of the centerpiece, as shown.
4. Children can decorate their centerpieces by attaching glitter, stickers, colored paper scraps, and other materials to the remaining three sides of the carton.

67

Centerpiece Pattern

Newbridge 68

Centerpiece Pattern

Newbridge

Centerpiece Pattern

Newbridge 70

Math Skills

THANKSGIVING MATH

You need:
- crayons or markers
- oaktag
- glue
- scissors

1. Organize children into groups of two, three, or four.
2. Reproduce all patterns on pages 68 through 70 many times for each group. Have children color, mount on oaktag, and cut out.
3. Demonstrate an addition or subtraction problem using the patterns as manipulatives. For example:
   If you have 3 bears and then get 5 more, how many bears will you have in all?
   If you have 9 turkeys and then give away 4, how many turkeys will you have left?
4. Encourage children to make up their own math word problems using the patterns as manipulatives. Invite them to give their problems to group members, who can use the patterns as an aid in figuring out the answers.

Self-Expression/Art/Oral Communication

WE ARE GRATEFUL

You need:
- a large sheet of oaktag or chart paper
- drawing paper
- crayons or markers

1. Remind children that Thanksgiving is a time to be thankful for the good things they have. Encourage children to talk about the different things they are grateful for.
2. Record all responses on a response chart similar to the one below.
3. After the response chart is complete, invite children to draw pictures showing what they are grateful for. Invite children to share their artwork with classmates if they wish.

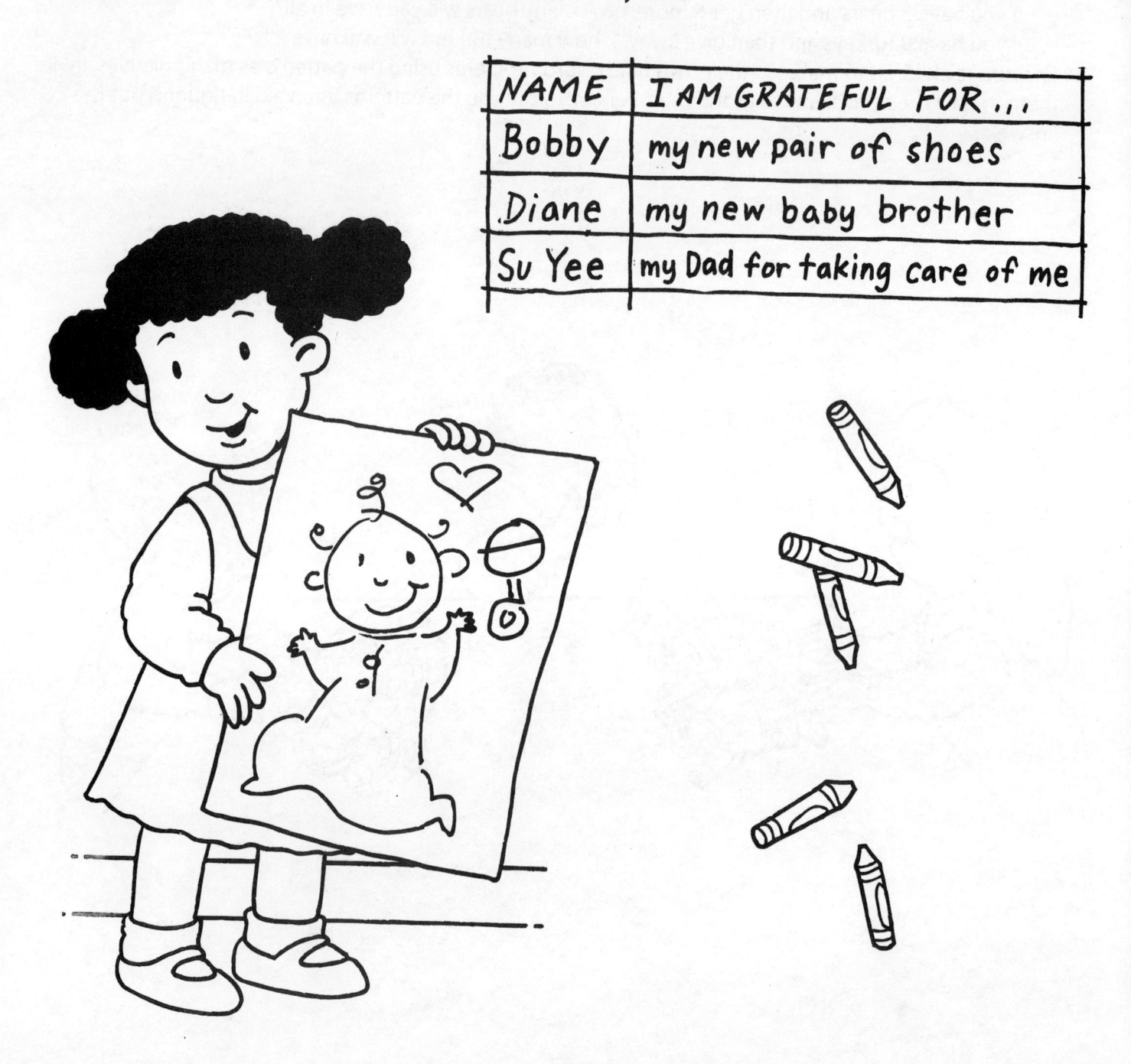

NAME	I AM GRATEFUL FOR...
Bobby	my new pair of shoes
Diane	my new baby brother
Su Yee	my Dad for taking care of me

Literature Connection/Listening Skills

WHY TREES TREMBLE IN THE WIND
FLANNEL BOARD STORY

Long ago there lived a Native American man who was the bravest, fastest, and best hunter in his tribe. The time had come for him to marry, and every maiden in his village wished to become his wife. When the man would return from hunting in the woods, he would visit many of the women. They all spoke such sweet words to him, and they were all beautiful. How would he choose which young woman to make his wife?

One day the man decided to visit his uncle, the Medicine Man in his tribe. It is said that the Medicine Man had great powers of magic, and could change people into different forms if he wished. The man talked with his uncle for a while, and told him of his difficulties in finding the best wife. The Medicine Man thought and thought, and soon he had a plan.

Out of the Medicine Man's home stepped an ugly, bent-over man wearing rags. It was the brave hunter in disguise! He walked around the village and visited all the beautiful maidens, asking for food and warmth from their fires. But not one of the women would invite him inside. Not one of the women would even look at him.

The ragged man went to one more home at the edge of the village. He was feeling very sad and lonely. As he came near the home, he saw two beautiful maidens sitting outside. They shrieked with laughter when he asked for food and told him to go away. They even threw rocks at him! But from the doorway, the man saw another beautiful face. This maiden took his hand to come inside and get warm. Her sisters shrieked again with laughter. They followed the man inside, talking about how ugly and stupid he looked. "Why should we waste our time and our food on this man?" they asked. "He can never give us anything."

The maiden helped the man sit by the fire and brought him some food. She even gave him a blanket she had made herself. The other sisters sat together, whispering, giggling, and pointing at the man. Finally they told him to get out of their home. The man hurried out the door.

When the ragged man returned to the Medicine Man's home, he was changed back into his handsome self. He sat by the fire and told his uncle the sad story of his afternoon spent wandering, and of the two maidens who had laughed and thrown rocks at him. The hunter's face brightened when he talked of the beautiful woman who had helped him. He held the blanket she had given him.

"You have found your wife at last," said the Medicine Man, although he was very angry about the mean women.

The brave hunter and his uncle visited the home of the three sisters once more. This time all the girls smiled and said kind things. But when they saw the blanket that belonged to the kind maiden, they knew the truth. The Medicine Man changed the two mean women into trees. Then he changed himself into a strong and gusty wind that shook the trees as he went on his way.

The brave hunter and the beautiful maiden were married soon after and lived a very happy life. But forever after, trees shiver and shake whenever there is a strong wind about, to remind people of the Medicine Man and the two mean sisters.

Listening Comprehension/Dramatic Play/Small Motor Skills/Art

HOW TO MAKE THE FLANNEL BOARD

You need:
- crayons or markers
- glue
- oaktag
- scissors
- sandpaper scraps

1. Reproduce the story patterns on pages 75 through 77 once. Have volunteers color the figures, mount on oaktag, and cut out.
2. Glue small sandpaper scraps to the backs of the figures.
3. Move the figures around the flannel board while reading the story on page 73.
4. Place the flannel board figures where children can use them to dramatize the story again during free time. Encourage children to make up stories of their own featuring the story characters.

NATIVE AMERICAN VILLAGE

You need:
- crayons or markers
- glue
- oaktag
- scissors

1. Reproduce the flannel board patterns several times each. Have children color, mount on oaktag, and cut out.
2. Give children small strips of oaktag to use as tabs. Children can glue the tabs to the backs of the figures so they can stand.
3. Let children place the Native Americans, tepees, and trees on a table, or designate an area on the floor to create their own Native American villages.
4. Have small groups of children make up stories about life in a Native American village. Encourage children to share their stories with the rest of the class.

Flannel Board Patterns

Newbridge

75

Flannel Board Patterns

Newbridge 76

Flannel Board Patterns

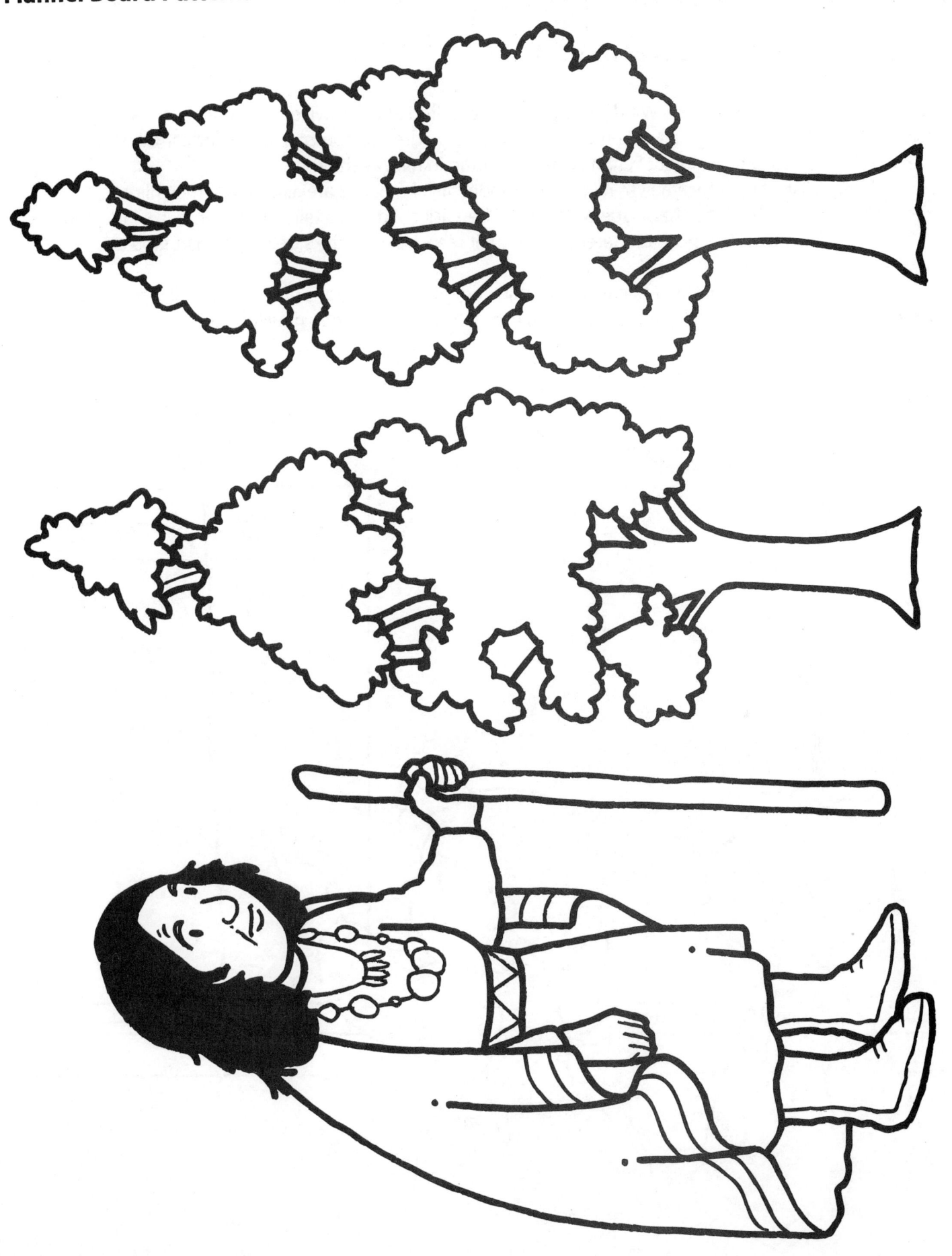

Newbridge 77

Listening Comprehension/Comparing and Contrasting/Creative Storytelling

CINDERELLA STORY CLASS DISCUSSION

1. Read "Why Trees Tremble in the Wind" on page 73 to children at least twice. Then read the traditional Cinderella tale, which is originally a French fairy tale. Ask children to compare and contrast the stories.
2. Make a chart by dividing a sheet of chart paper or oaktag in half, as shown.
3. Have children list all the ways they think the two Cinderella characters are alike. Write the children's responses on the side of the chard labeled "Same." Then ask children to tell how the French Cinderella differs from the Native American Cinderella. Write their responses on the side of the chart labeled "Different."
4. After discussing the two stories, ask children to think up different versions of the Cinderella story. Have children write or dictate their stories, and then illustrate scenes from their new folktales.

SAME	DIFFERENT
PRETTY	CLOTHES
KIND	HOUSE

Thinking Skills/Cooperative Play

GUESSING GAME
(adapted from a Northwest Coast Indian game)

1. Ask a small group of children to sit in a circle.
2. Display such objects as pinecones, different types of leaves, seeds, berries, and Indian corn on a tray or in a shallow box. Discuss each of the objects with children.
3. Put the tray or box in the center of the circle. Allow the children 30 seconds to look closely at the array of objects.
4. Remove the objects from view. Choose one child to secretly take one of the objects and hold it behind his or her back.
5. Encourage the rest of the children to ask questions about the hidden object, such as "Is it big?" or "Is it red?" and so on.
6. The child holding the object may answer each question only yes or no. The child who correctly guesses the object becomes the next one to hide a different object.

Teacher's Notes